HAL•LEONARD
INSTRUMENTAL PLAY-ALONG

AUDIO ACCESS INCLUDED

PLAYBACK+
Speed • Pitch • Balance • Loop

HORN

TOP HITS

T0070704

Audio arrangements by Peter Deneff

To access audio visit:
www.halleonard.com/mylibrary

Enter Code
4096-5017-4905-2125

ISBN 978-1-4950-6577-4

HAL•LEONARD®
CORPORATION

7777 W. BLUEMOUND RD. P.O. BOX 13819 MILWAUKEE, WI 53213

Visit Hal Leonard Online at
www.halleonard.com

ADVENTURE OF A LIFETIME

Horn

Words and Music by GUY BERRYMAN,
JON BUCKLAND, CHRIS MARTIN,
WILL CHAMPION, MIKKEL ERIKSEN
and TOR HERMANSEN

BUDAPEST

HORN

Words and Music by GEORGE BARNETT
and JOEL POTT

To Coda $\oplus$

D.S. al Coda
(no repeat)

CODA
$\oplus$

mf

DIE A HAPPY MAN

Horn

Words and Music by THOMAS RHETT,
JOE SPARGUR and SEAN DOUGLAS

To Coda ⊕ **7**

D.S. al Coda

CODA ⊕

mf

mp *rit.*

EX'S & OH'S

Horn

Words and Music by TANNER SCHNEIDER
and DAVE BASSETT

FIGHT SONG

Horn

Words and Music by RACHEL PLATTEN
and DAVE BASSETT

D.S. al Coda

CODA

HELLO

HORN

Words and Music by ADELE ADKINS
and GREG KURSTIN

To Coda ⊕

D.S. al Coda

mp

CODA
⊕

1.

2.

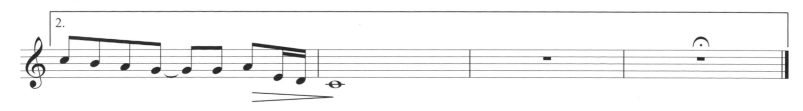

LET IT GO

HORN

Words and Music by JAMES BAY
and PAUL BARRY

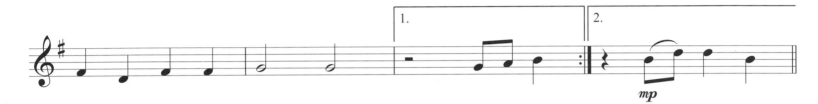

LOVE YOURSELF

Horn

Words and Music by JUSTIN BIEBER,
BENJAMIN LEVIN and ED SHEERAN

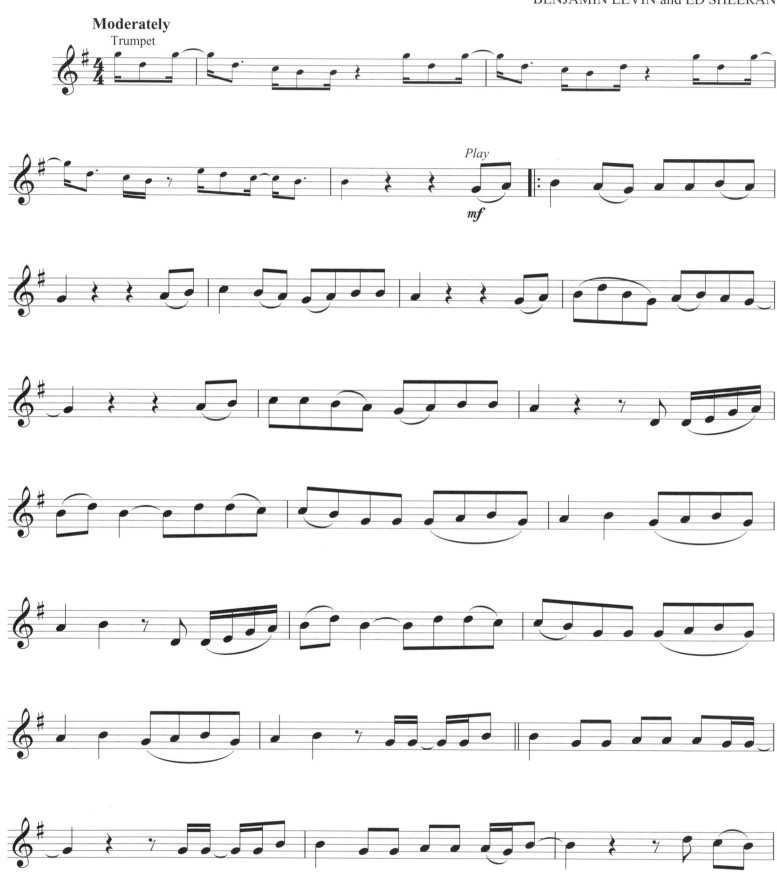

ONE CALL AWAY

Horn

Words and Music by CHARLIE PUTH,
BREYAN ISAAC, MATT PRIME,
JUSTIN FRANKS, BLAKE ANTHONY CARTER
and MAUREEN McDONALD

PILLOWTALK

Horn

Words and Music by LEVI LENNOX,
ANTHONY HANNIDES, MICHAEL HANNIDES,
ZAYN MALIK and JOE GARRETT

To Coda

D.S. al Coda
(take 3rd ending)

CODA

STITCHES

HORN

Words and Music by TEDDY GEIGER,
DANNY PARKER and DANIEL KYRIAKIDES

To Coda ⊕   **D.S. al Coda**

CODA ⊕

4

1.   2.

WRITING'S ON THE WALL

from the film SPECTRE

Horn

Words and Music by SAM SMITH
and JAMES NAPIER